BUTTERFLY
Album
MONARCHS & MORE

BEA OGLESBY

American Quilter's Society

P. O. Box 3290 • Paducah, KY 42002-3290

www.AmericanQuilter.com

Located in Paducah, Kentucky, the American Quilter's Society (AQS) is dedicated to promoting the accomplishments of today's quilters. Through its publications and events, AQS strives to honor today's quiltmakers and their work and to inspire future creativity and innovation in quiltmaking.

EDITOR: BARBARA SMITH
GRAPHIC DESIGN: ELAINE WILSON
COVER DESIGN: MICHAEL BUCKINGHAM
PHOTOGRAPHY: CHARLES R. LYNCH

Library of Congress Cataloging-in-Publication Data

Oglesby, Bea, 1924-

   Butterfly album : monarchs & more / by Bea Oglesby.

     p. cm.

   Includes bibliographical references and index.

   ISBN 1-57432-871-9 (alk. paper)

  1. Appliqué--Patterns. 2. Embroidery--Patterns. 3. Quilting--Patterns. I. Title.

TT779.03323 2005

746.44'5--dc22

                         2004022245

Additional copies of this book may be ordered from the American Quilter's Society, PO Box 3290, Paducah, KY 42002-3290; 800-626-5420 (orders only please); or online at www.AmericanQuilter.com. For all other inquiries, call 270-898-7903.

DEDICATION

To my eight grandchildren, Marie-Therese, Thomas, Michael, Emily, Bill, Dan, Colin, and Katie, with the hope that they will appreciate nature's glory and see beauty in all that surrounds us.

BUTTERFLIES AND WILDFLOWERS, 17"x 22", made by the author

ACKNOWLEDGMENTS

Thank you ...

To my husband, Red, for his assistance in my research on the butterflies.

To my friends and shop owners, Debbie Richards of Quilters' Haven, Carol Kirchhoff of Prairie Point, and Julie Kiffin of Liberty Quilt Shop, for their inspiration, guidance, and help with fabric choices and their patience in assisting me.

To my quilting students, who, with their enthusiasm, have encouraged me to continue with my drawing, writing, and quilting.

To Barbara Smith and the special people at the American Quilter's Society for their support in making this book a reality.

BUTTERFLIES ARE FREE, 39"x 30", made by the author

CONTENTS

PREFACE

Welcome to the wonderful world of butterflies. We plant our gardens to give us colorful flowers. We watch, water, and feed our birds, but it is the butterflies that offer us such a vast variety of extraordinary and colorful patterns and an interesting life history in our natural world. I became interested in watching butterflies as a result of my interest in wildflowers and birds. It is difficult not to discover butterflies while planting flowers and watching birds because they all interact together. They complement the flowers both cultivated and wild, and they are more diverse than birds and much easier to approach for close observation and study.

Butterflies have impressed themselves on man's imagination for centuries. They have been the subject of art from the earliest of times and were a fascination for the ancient artists of China, Korea, and Japan. After the Renaissance, nature was rediscovered in our Western world, and English poets celebrated the beauty of butterflies. In the nineteenth century, there were many references to butterflies in American prose and poetry. In our own modern world, we see butterflies used in décor all around us. They are popular in our fabrics and as designs in pottery, china, note paper, greeting cards, and art. In quiltmaking, butterflies have long been a favorite design, and they can be found on antique as well as contemporary quilts.

The name "butterfly" was first given to the European brimstone butterfly, whose rich yellow color reminded the peasants of butter. Not all butterflies are brightly colored. Many are tan, brown, or gray. The most colorful ones are in South America and in the tropics, but here in North America, we do enjoy a full rainbow of colors. There are variations in the colors and markings within species, and some species will change dramatically in color between the seasons. On some species, the markings and colors on the forewings differ from those on the hind wings. Some butterflies are masters of disguise, and while at rest, may resemble tree bark or a leaf.

The disappearance of butterflies from our gardens would mean not only a loss of beauty for us to observe, but also a great loss to our flowers that rely on them for pollination. The most dangerous enemy of the butterfly is mankind, and every year with more development, there are fewer wild places for them on this Earth. The use of pesticides and the existence of pollution are also serious threats to them, and global warming is causing problems with the migration of the monarchs.

We can all help in the conservation of butterflies by using native plants and flowers in our landscaping. We can also introduce flowers that attract butterflies in our own gardens. There is a wealth of material about butterfly gardens in our local libraries. After World War II, Sir Winston Churchill planted a butterfly garden, and many cities have butterfly gardens for us to visit. My garden is rather careless and without too much order, but my butterflies do not complain and even seem to enjoy my mix of annuals, perennials, and wildflowers. With a little effort on our part, we can have the pleasure of enjoying our native butterflies and be a host to those who migrate through our states. Watching butterflies is an extension of my love of nature and has given me many hours of joy. So, welcome to my wonderful world of butterflies.

INTRODUCTION

After completing my first books, *Wildflower Album* and *Birds and Flowers Album*, I felt that the next step was butterflies. Watching them in nature, I was intimidated by their beauty and did not feel that I could do them justice. After doing research in our local library, I discovered that the basic butterfly was composed of a body, two forewings, and two hind wings, so I started drawing. I chose North American butterflies, most of which I have seen either in Kansas or in other areas of the country where I have lived. I have chosen for my patterns different groups of butterflies with one to five examples in each group. I also have several monarch butterfly patterns with different sizes and shapes. I do not think that I did them justice; however, I enjoyed much pleasure in the research, study, drawing, and appliquéing of these butterflies.

My butterflies were appliquéd onto an eight-inch background square. I used no sashing, but sewed the background blocks together randomly with some four-by-eight-inch filler blocks so the butterflies could "fly free." Each pattern can be used by itself or with a favorite flower or combined with butterflies of the same group or mixed with other groups. I have done them in several ways. This can be your personal choice.

The patterns are not too difficult, varying from three pieces in the checkered white butterfly up to 25 pieces in the zebra swallowtail. Most of the patterns have five to nine pieces to appliqué. Many of the butterfly patterns have been simplified for appliqué; however, I was true to the basic shape and markings of the individual butterflies in my drawings. The fabrics I chose were basically the colors of the species, but I may have chosen some brighter fabrics for contrast. Also, if the butterfly had different colorings for spring and fall, I chose what I desired.

If you are new to quilting and appliqué, it would be wise to take a basic class to learn your skills. My butterflies were hand appliquéd with freezer-paper patterns and the needle-turn method. They could be done with fusible web if desired. I used embroidery for all the antennae and for some of the markings on their wings. I also used both permanent marking pens and brush tip pens for some of the markings. Brush tip pens come in a set of eight different colors, and the marking pens come in different colors and sizes. The veins in the butterfly wings are a part of their beauty. Some of these veins are the same shade as the wing and some are in bold contrast. The pens were used to mark the veins, and then they were quilted in that color.

For each of the 37 butterflies, there is a color photograph of the block, a full-sized pattern, and tips on appliqué and fabric selection. Also included are a description and characteristics of the individual butterflies.

MONARCHS AND MORE, 66"x 74", made by the author

BUTTERFLY INSTRUCTIONS

There are several techniques for hand appliqué. If you have a favorite method, by all means use it. Sometimes it is good to try a different technique so that you are able to understand the various methods. Some methods are not suited for all appliqué quilt projects. These basic instructions will offer a brief introduction to my method of appliquéing the butterflies.

On the large quilt, MONARCHS AND MORE, each butterfly was appliquéd onto an eight-inch square. These were randomly set together with some blank eight-inch and some four-by-eight-inch blocks. With the three borders added, I obtained the desired size. On the wallhanging BUTTERFLIES ARE FREE, I appliquéd five different butterflies on a field of coneflowers. With the addition of the border, I have a wallhanging 39 inches by 30 inches. Use your imagination and experiment with these butterfly patterns. They can be used singly for a pillow or a small wallhanging or combined in a variety of ways.

SUPPLIES

With appliqué, your supplies are basic. You probably already have them in your sewing box. If they are not of the best quality, I would suggest replacing them, because minimal equipment is needed for appliqué and the proper tools can help you to be successful. I recommend the following basic supplies:

Freezer paper (coated with plastic). For accurate butterfly patterns.

Needles. Size 11 or 12. The smaller the needle, the smaller and finer the stitch.

Thread. Cotton #60 or silk that matches the appliqué. The finer the thread, the more invisible the stitch.

Thimble. A metal thimble with dimples to keep the needle from slipping.

Pins. Silk pins with glass heads, or small appliqué pins with glass heads.

Scissors. Two pair, one for fabric and one for paper.

Markers. Pencils, chalk markers of different colors, super-thin-lead quilter's mechanical pencil. Markers can be your personal choice. If it is a washout marker, test it first on your chosen fabric to be sure it does wash out. For permanent markers, I use the Pigma® Micron® permanent marker and the Pigma brush tip pens.

Iron and ironing board. Be sure to press your fabrics before you cut them.

BACKGROUND FABRIC

Use 100 percent cotton that is prewashed and ironed for the background fabric. Use an overall discreet or muted pattern so as not to distract from the butterflies. If you plan on a small wallhanging with only a few butterflies, you can choose a background color that will contrast with the chosen butterflies.

APPLIQUÉ FABRIC

Use 100 percent cotton. Cotton has a memory. It keeps a crease where it has been finger pressed so it is easy to work with. Best of all, cotton is available in a great variety of colors, styles, and patterns. As you look for fabric for the different butterfly wings, you will find yourself looking at not only color but also the design and scale on the fabric. To help in choosing some of the fabric for the butterfly wings, I make a window template of the wing. The template assists me in blocking out the whole bolt of fabric, and I am able to see exactly how that small butterfly wing will look.

APPLIQUÉ METHOD

After the background fabric has been washed and dried, cut the background 2" larger than the size of your finished piece. The appliqué often draws up the fabric, and the edges fray. The block will be trimmed to size when the appliqué is finished. Spray the background with starch and iron it dry. Starch gives the fabric body and makes it easier to mark and to sew.

Place the background fabric over the pattern and mark the complete pattern with a washout marker or with a quilter's mechanical pencil. If your fabric is dark, you may need a light box to see the pattern.

To make the butterfly templates, use a pencil to draw the pattern on the dull side of freezer paper. Mark each pattern piece with its number and cut the pattern pieces out exactly on the line. Do not add seam allowances to the templates.

Position the templates on the right side of the desired fabric and press in place with a dry iron. Mark around each piece with a wash-out marker. This will be your sewing line. Cut out these pieces, leaving a turn-under allowance of ¼". If necessary, the allowance can be trimmed narrower as you appliqué.

Starting with piece 1, with the freezer paper still in place, turn the allowance to the back and finger press the fabric on the sewing line. By using cotton fabric, the crease will remain and the seam allowance will easily needle-turn with the appliqué stitch. Remove the freezer paper and place the fabric appliqué piece in its place on the background. The piece can be held in place with one pin. On large curves, the turn-under allowance may need to be trimmed closer to the fold as you sew. With tiny, close stitches, appliqué around this first piece. Continue adding pieces in numerical order.

With many of the butterflies, there are narrow edges on the wings. I found that it is easier to sew these pieces together as a unit off the background and treat the unit as one piece before sewing it on the background. I have made notes in the individual butterfly tips when I used this method.

After the appliqué is finished, embroider the antennae and mark the veins in the wings with a permanent marker. Wash out any pattern markings that show. Press and trim the background to size for your block or wallhanging.

PATTERNS

MIGRATION, 27"x 32", made by the author

MONARCHS

Size 3½" to 4"

This regal, beautiful creature is probably the most famous North American butterfly, and it deserves its name. Most of the species are found in tropical Asia, but the ones in North America include the monarch, the queen, and the tropical queen. These are all similar in appearance.

• • • • • • • • • • • • • • • • • • • •

Monarch 1

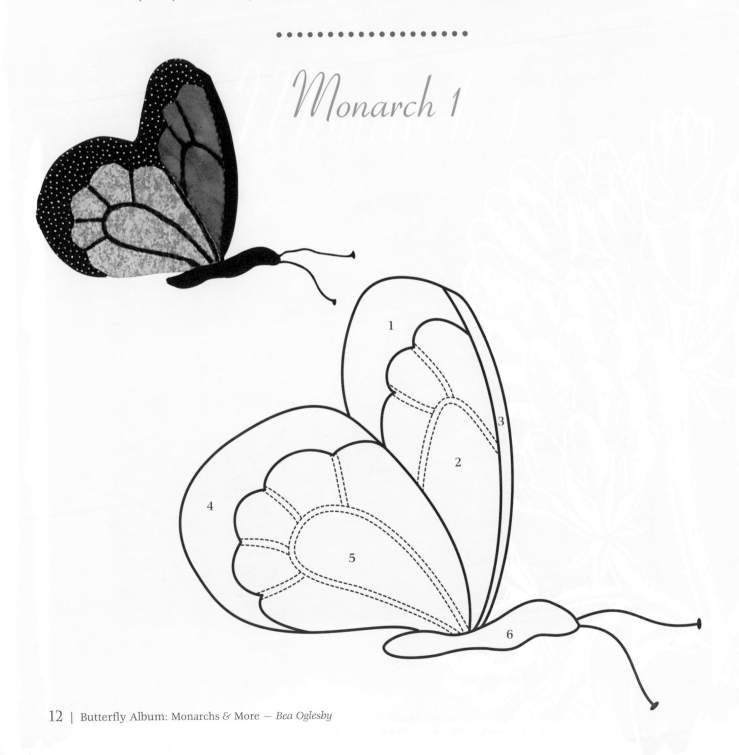

Monarch 2

The monarch's wings are large. Its coloring is bright orange with black veins and black edges that are sprinkled with white dots. The forewings are a deeper shade than the hind wings.

Its range is all of North America except for northern Canada and northern Alaska. The monarch is best known for its migration from Canada to Mexico. Where I live in Kansas, we can observe them over several weeks, usually peaking in September and early October. The far western and Sierra Nevada monarchs are exceptional because they migrate only between central and southern California.

The host plant is the milkweed. It is toxic, and as a result, the adult monarchs are distasteful to birds, giving the butterflies some protection from predators. This butterfly is a welcome guest in our gardens and is one of the few butterflies most people know by name.

6 –13 APPLIQUÉ PIECES

COLOR NOTES

I chose two oranges, one dark and one light, for the wings. I used black for the body and for the trim, and a black-and-white dotted fabric for the wing edges.

CONSTRUCTION TIPS

Each of the wings was sewn off the background then appliquéd as one unit.

DETAILS

White wing spots: satin stitched with two strands of white floss

Antennae: stem stitched with two strands of black floss

Veins: drawn with black marker, then quilted in black quilting thread

Monarch 3

Monarch 4

Monarch 9

SKIPPERS

There are approximately 250 species of skippers in North America. These butterflies were so named because of their rapid and skipping flight. Their species names were given because of their markings, colors, or host plants. True skippers are usually medium in size and have broad heads, hairy bodies, and long triangular wings. There are three sub-families of skippers. One family basks in the sun with its wings folded back, and one suns with its wings spread. The third family is a subtropical group spotted with red.

• • • • • • • • • • • • • • • • • • •

Arsalte Skipper

Size 1¼" to 1½"

This is a small skipper also known as the veined white skipper. The body is a creamy white mottled with tan. It is edged with dark brown or brownish black. There is not much information on this butterfly, because it was not discovered in the United States until 1973, in Brownsville, Texas.

Its range is Mexico and South America, and in the fall, it comes north to south Texas. Its life cycle is unknown, but it is believed that its hosts are desert plants.

9 APPLIQUÉ PIECES

COLOR NOTES

I used a marbled creamy white for the wings and dark brown for the edges and body.

DETAILS

Antennae: stem stitched with two strands of brown floss

Veins: quilted in light brown quilting thread

Arsalte Skipper

Sickle-Winged Skipper

Size 1½" to almost 2"

The sickle-winged skipper has full rounded wings with slight hooks on the forewing tips. Its forewings are black with wide dark purple edges. Its hind wings are dark purple with black edges. The body is black. With these hooked tips and the violet sheen, this skipper is distinct from other skippers.

The sickle-winged skipper lives year-round in Texas and in South America. Its hosts include all kinds of citrus plants.

11 APPLIQUÉ PIECES

COLOR NOTES

I used two fabrics, a black and a deep mottled purple.

CONSTRUCTION TIPS

If you desire, the hind wings can be sewn off the background. Then each wing is treated as a unit and appliquéd in place.

DETAILS

Antennae: stem stitched with two strands of black floss

Veins: quilted with dark purple quilting thread

Guava Skipper

Guava Skipper

This is a tropical butterfly that has long wings drawn out at the tip. It is dark gray and black with metallic green on the forewings. Both the forewings and the hind wings are edged with white. There is a scarlet red patch on the forewings, which marks it as a subtropical skipper. The body is a deeper gray.

It ranges from south Texas to Mexico and South America. The host plant is the guava tree, thus the name.

9 APPLIQUÉ PIECES

COLOR NOTES

I used a medium gray for the hind wings, greenish-gray for the forewings, dark gray for the body, and white for the edges.

CONSTRUCTION TIPS

Each of the wings was sewn off the background then appliquéd as one unit.

DETAILS

Red patches: satin stitched with two strands of red floss

Antennae: stem stitched with two strands of dark gray floss

Veins: quilted with dark gray quilting thread

Golden-Banded

Size 1½" to 2"

This dramatic and beautiful butterfly is a true spread-winged skipper. Its forewings, hind wings, and body are a deep brownish black. The forewings have wide, golden bands across them and a small white dot near the tip of each one. They are easily spotted because of their coloring as they search for nectar in our gardens.

Many of these attractive skippers are found only in the southern states, but this one goes well into the Northeast from New York south to northern Florida and west to Arizona and New Mexico. Their host plant is the hog peanut.

11 APPLIQUÉ PIECES

COLOR NOTES

I used a brownish black fabric for the wings and body, gold for the bands, and white for hind wing edges.

DETAILS

White wing spots: satin stitched with two strands of white floss

Antennae: stem stitched with two strands of black floss

Veins: quilted in gray quilting thread

Golden-Banded Skipper

SULPHURS

The sulphurs are easy to spot because of their coloring, which ranges from pale yellow to bright yellow, orange, and yellowish green. Many species' wings are edged with a black or brown border. Others have pink fringes and spots on their wings.

The most common species are found in open meadows, fields, and parks. The less common species are found in mountains and colder regions.

. . . .

Southern Dogface

Southern Dogface

Size 2" to 2½"

It gets its name from the pattern on the topside of its forewings. When the wings are open, the design resembles the profile of a poodle, with a black spot that suggests an eye. The butterflies are mostly yellow with wings edged in a deeper shade or a reddish brown. The spots on the underside of the wings are also reddish brown.

They prefer warmer climates, and although they do go north into the Midwest, they are more abundant in California, Texas, and north Florida. Their host plants are false indigo, legumes, and clovers.

7 APPLIQUÉ PIECES

COLOR NOTES
I used a medium shade of yellow for the wings and a reddish brown for the wing edges and the body.

CONSTRUCTION TIPS
After I appliquéd the body (piece #1) on the background, I reverse appliquéd spots #2 and #3.

The easiest way to do the narrow brown edges is to sew the yellow wing pieces to the edges to make units, then appliqué the units to the background.

DETAILS
Small spots: marked with a brown pen

Antennae: stem stitched with two strands of floss that matches the body

Veins: quilted in yellow quilting thread

Orange Sulphur

Size 1¾" to 2¾"

These butterflies are very bright in color. The forewings have a golden orange cast to them, and the hind wings have a greenish yellow cast. They have a wide black border on both sets of wings and a large black spot on the forewings. Orange sulphurs will hybridize with other sulphurs, which produces many part-orange or part-yellow butterflies. This can make them difficult to identify.

They range throughout the United States but are rare in the Far North and in subtropical Florida. They have a taste for garden and farm plants, and their host plants include legumes, alfalfa, and white clover.

9 APPLIQUÉ PIECES

COLOR NOTES
I used a medium yellow for the wings and black for the wing edges and body.

CONSTRUCTION TIPS
To give the wings an orange and greenish cast, I lined the forewings with an orange fabric and the hind wings with a green fabric. These linings were cut a scant smaller than the pattern and were basted in place before the yellow wing pieces were appliquéd.

The black spots were appliquéd after the wings were in place, however the spots can be embroidered with black floss in the satin stitch, if desired.

DETAILS
Antennae: stem stitched with two strands of black floss

Veins: quilted in yellow quilting thread

Orange Sulphur

Sleepy Orange

Size 1¼" to 1¾"

Both the forewings and hind wings are bright golden orange. The hind wings are a little darker. The wings are edged with a distinct and uneven border of cocoa brown, and the bodies are dark cocoa brown. The name may have come about because they do not tolerate the cold. On cooler days, this butterfly has a habit of hibernating, which gives the appearance of being asleep. In warm weather, with their rapid flight, they seem anything but sleepy.

They range throughout the South and east of the Rockies. They rarely go into the Northeast and are prolific in the South. Host plants include clovers and legumes.

9 APPLIQUÉ PIECES

COLOR NOTES

I used a bright orange mottled batik fabric for the wings and a dark brown for the wing edges and the body.

DETAILS

Antennae: stem stitched with two strands of dark brown floss

Veins: quilted in gold quilting thread

Pink-Edged Sulphur

Size 1¼" to 1¾"

This medium-sized yellow sulphur has rounded wings edged with bright pink. Both sexes have a deep gold spot on the forewings. The body is a deep gold. These sulphurs are better known than others in the sulphur family because of their distinctive coloring.

They are more tolerant of the cooler weather than the sleepy orange sulphur, and range from Newfoundland south to Virginia and as far west as Oregon. They enjoy meadows and open spaces but can also be found in marshes and bogs. Their host is the blueberry.

9 APPLIQUÉ PIECES

COLOR NOTES

I used a medium yellow for the wings, gold for the body and the spot, and bright pink for the edges.

CONSTRUCTION TIPS

I found it easy to sew the main wing pieces onto the pink edges, then treat the joined pieces as units for appliquéing in place. The spots were appliquéd after the wings.

DETAILS

Antennae: stem stitched with two strands of gold floss

Veins: quilted in dark gold quilting thread

WHITES

White butterflies are familiar to all of us, because they show up so well against the flowers and leaves in our gardens. Their wings are mainly white but can be yellowish in color with differences in their borders, spots, or splotches, which can be tan, brown, black, orange, or even greenish yellow.

• • • • • • • • • • • • • • • • • •

Checkered White

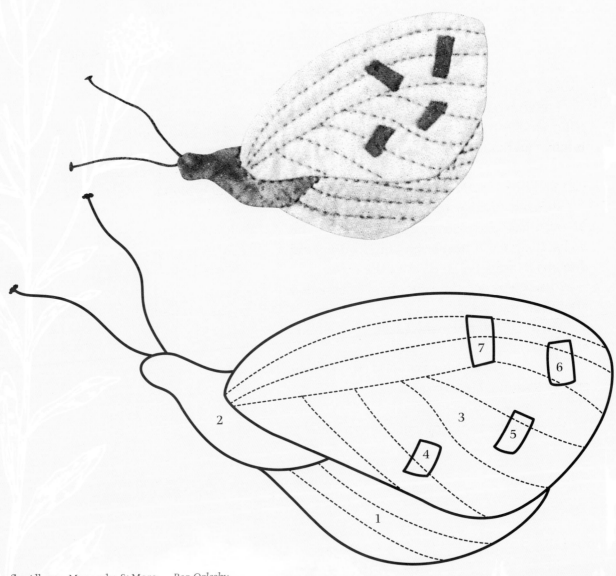

Checkered White

Size 1¼" to 1¾"

The checkered white is generally white; however, it can be shades of gray or beige or even a dull olive green. It is heavily checkered with charcoal on the forewings. It is not as numerous as the cabbage white, although it can reach enormous numbers. Many farmers confuse the two butterflies, but the checkered white does less damage to our gardens.

Its range is most of the United States except for the Northwest. Its host plants are local native plants including cabbage and mustard.

7 appliqué pieces

COLOR NOTES
I used two fabrics, a white-on-white for the wings and gray for the body. The upper wing is white and the body is gray.

CONSTRUCTION TIPS
To have a darker underwing, I lined piece #1 with the gray fabric that I used for the body. It shows through the white fabric and darkens it.

I used gray for the spots that I appliquéd after the wing was in place.

DETAILS
Antennae: stem stitched with two strands of gray floss

Veins: quilted with gray quilting thread

Cabbage White

Size 1½" to 2"

This butterfly is creamy white with black tips on the forewings and black spots on both forewings and hind wings. The body is black and the veins are prominent. It is considered a pest to farmers and gardeners because of its enormous appetite. Its host plants include many vegetables and flowers.

Its range covers all of North America from Alaska south to Mexico.

8 appliqué pieces

COLOR NOTES
I used a white-on-white fabric for the wings and black for the body and spots.

CONSTRUCTION TIP
The black spots were done in reverse appliqué. If you desire, these spots can be appliquéd after the wings have been sewn to the background.

DETAILS
Antennae: stem stitched with two strands of black floss

Veins: quilted in gray quilting thread

Cabbage White

Western Orangetip

Size 1½" to 1¾"

This butterfly is also known as the Sara orangetip. Although most of them are white, sometimes they are pale yellow. They have a brilliant red orange tip on each forewing with a black bar dividing the white from the orange. The hind wings are edged in black, and the body is black.

Their range is west of the Rockies from Alaska to Baja California. They are at home in aspen woods and meadows as well as desert canyons and arid slopes. Host plants include many kinds of crucifers and wild greens.

11 APPLIQUÉ PIECES

COLOR NOTES

I used a white-on-white for the wings, a mottled red orange for the wing tips, and black for the trim and the body.

CONSTRUCTION TIP

Each of the wings was sewn off the background then appliquéd as one unit.

DETAILS

Antennae: stem stitched with two strands of black floss

Veins: quilted in white quilting thread

Eastern Orangetip

Size 1¼" to 1½"

This butterfly is a bit smaller than the western orangetip. It is also known as the falcate orangetip. This is a familiar butterfly in the spring with its clear white wings. The male has a bright red orange triangle patch on the front edges of the forewings. The female lacks the bright orange but does have a pale orange flush on the forewing tips. The forewings and the hind wings of both the male and the female are edged in black. The body is black.

Their range is the eastern part of the United States from Massachusetts south to Georgia and west to Kansas and Texas. Their host plants are various wild greens including mustard and cabbage.

11 APPLIQUÉ PIECES

COLOR NOTES

A white-on-white fabric was used for the forewings and the hind wings, a bright orange for the triangle tips, and a dark gray for the body and wing edges.

DETAILS

Antennae: stem stitched with two strands of dark gray floss

Veins: quilted in dark gray quilting thread

Western Orangetip

Eastern Orangetip

FRITILLARIES

Fritillaries are recognized by their orange color and irregular wing markings. They are members of the large and diverse family of brush-footed butterflies. They have many of the same characteristics of the admirals, anglewings, leafwings, and longwings but differ in their colorings and markings. Most of the fritillaries are orange, ranging from a tawny beige, rust, and dull orange to a brilliant orange. The patterns on their wings are black in different designs of dots, veins, zigzags, crescents, and bars.

• • • • • • • • • • • • • • • • • •

Western Meadow

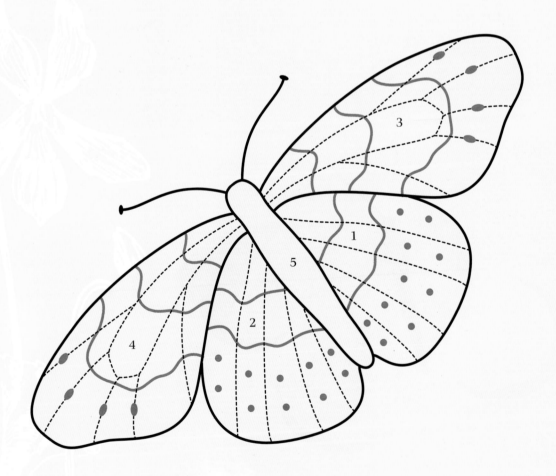

Western Meadow

Size 1¼" to 1½"

This small butterfly is typical of the fritillaries in its coloring and markings. The body and the rounded wings are rusty orange with heavily patterned markings in black on the upper side.

This butterfly is most abundant in the Northwest and ranges from western Canada south into northern California. This is the only fritillary that lives in both lowland and highland habitats. Violets are the host plants.

5 APPLIQUÉ PIECES

COLOR NOTES
I used only one rusty orange patterned fabric.

DETAILS
Lines and dots: drawn in black pen.

Antennae: stem stitched with two strands of rust floss.

Veins: quilted in rust quilting thread.

Julia

Julia

Size 3¼" to 3¾"

This is a large butterfly with long, narrow wings. The Julia is a clear, bright butterfly with boldly marked black veins and black bars on its forewings. Because of its brilliant coloring, it is easy to spot.

Its range is the American tropics, south Texas, and south Florida. It can be extremely abundant in the Florida Keys. The host plant is the passion flower.

5 APPLIQUÉ PIECES

COLOR NOTES

I used two shades of orange for the wings, a brighter orange for the forewings, and a duller shade for the hind wings. A tawny, dull orange was used for the body.

DETAILS

Antennae: stem stitched in two strands of dull gold floss that matches the body

Bars: marked with black pen

Veins: marked with black pen then quilted in black quilting thread

Diana

Size 3" to 4"

This is also a large butterfly. The Diana fits into several categories and is included in the fritillaries, the boldly patterned, and the brush-footed families. This butterfly has large rounded wings that are brownish black. One third of the wing is edged in a bright orange heavily marked with black spots. The body is brownish black. The Diana is considered the most beautiful fritillary.

Its range is the eastern part of the United States west to Illinois and south to Georgia. Violets are the host plants.

9 APPLIQUÉ PIECES

COLOR NOTES

I used a brownish black for the wings and the body and a bright orange for the edges.

DETAILS

Lines and dots: drawn in black pen

Antennae: stem stitched with two strands of black floss

Diana

BOLDLY PATTERNED

This group of butterflies is just what the name implies. They are patterned with bright and bold stripes, spots, or patches across the upper side of the wings.

• • • • • • • • • • • • • • • • • •

American Painted Lady

Painted Lady

Size 1¾" to 2"

This is also called hunter's butterfly and Virginia lady. It is basically orange and black, but the orange is a salmon or golden shade of orange. The wings are edged in black, and the body is a deeper shade than the wings.

Its range is the eastern part of the United States south to Mexico. They have a great fondness for our garden flowers and are regular visitors to them. Their host plants are various species of everlastings.

9 APPLIQUÉ PIECES

COLOR NOTES

I used two shades of a golden orange for the wings. The hind wings are a darker shade than the forewings. A deeper shade was used for the body and black for the edges.

CONSTRUCTION TIP

The hind wings and edges were sewn off the background and then appliquéd as one unit.

DETAILS

Antennae: stem stitched with two strands of black floss

Veins: quilted in black quilting thread

Red Admiral

Size approximately 2" to 2¼"

It is easily noticed in the fields because of its unique coloring. The forewings are a rich black that looks like velvet. They have a bright red bar across these wings, and the edges have white spots. The hind wings are also black and banded with red. There are two bright blue patches or dots on the inside edges of the hind wings. The body is black.

It ranges throughout the United States as far north as Alaska and south into Mexico. The red admiral can be found in gardens, parks, meadows, and fields, and it is fond of the nectar from fermented fruit. Nettles are their main host plants.

11 APPLIQUÉ PIECES

COLOR NOTES

I used black and red for this butterfly.

DETAILS

Spots: satin stitched with two strands of white floss and two strands of blue floss

Antennae: stem stitched with two strands of black floss

Veins: quilted in black quilting thread

Red Admiral

Malachite

Size 2½" to 3"

The malachite is boldly patterned and dramatic in black and green. The green in these butterflies ranges from pale jade to deep emerald. The forewings are black and spotted with green. The scalloped hind wings have a tail and two broad green bands.

This is a tropical butterfly that ranges from south Texas and south Florida into South America. It loves thick woodlands. They are not numerous, but more sightings have occurred recently in Florida. Tropical plants are their hosts.

19 APPLIQUÉ PIECES

COLOR NOTES

Two fabrics were used, a black and a jade green.

CONSTRUCTION TIP

The large oval spots were appliquéd onto the wings after they were sewn to the background.

DETAILS

Antennae: stem stitched with two strands of black floss

Veins: quilted in black quilting thread

Mourning Cloak

Size 3" to 3½"

This is an exotic-looking butterfly with unmistakable colorings. Its wings are rich, deep maroon with yellow edges and a band of blue dots between the maroon and the yellow. The undersides of the wings are a dull brown, resembling dirt or tree bark. While these butterflies are at rest, they are almost impossible to see.

Their range covers almost all of the United States from Alaska into Mexico. Their host plants include willows, elms, and cottonwood.

13 APPLIQUÉ PIECES

COLOR NOTES

I used a brownish maroon for the wings and the body. A bright yellow was used for the edges and bright blue for the bands.

DETAILS

Antennae: stem stitched with two strands of floss that match the body

Veins: quilted in brown quilting thread

Crimson-Patched Longwing

Size 3" to 3½"

It is aptly named with its long, narrow, rounded wings. The wings are black, and the forewings are crossed with a wide crimson patch. There is a narrow, bright yellow line on the upper part of the hind wing. This butterfly flies low over the ground, showing off its bright coloring.

The range is south Texas to South America. The host plant is the passion flower.

11 APPLIQUÉ PIECES

COLOR NOTES

I used black, crimson, and bright yellow fabrics.

DETAILS

Antennae: stem stitched with two strands of black floss

Veins: quilted in black quilting thread

ANGLEWINGS

These butterflies belong to the large brush-footed family. They are called anglewings because their irregular wings are sharply angled. The upper sides of the wings are brightly colored, from red orange to rust to a rusty brown. On the underside, they are drab brown so that, while at rest with the wings folded back, they resemble tree bark. This camouflage makes it difficult for predators to see them.

• • • • • • • • • • • • • • • • • •

Question Mark

Question Mark Ruddy Daggerwing

Size 2¼" to 2½"

The question mark is distinct in its coloring, which changes with the seasons. The butterfly is shown in its fall coloring. The forewings are rust with blotches of black. These wings have a black band edged with violet. The hind wings are black, edged in violet. The body is also black. The wings are rather ragged looking, and they have a small tail. There is a marking on the underside of the hind wing that resembles a question mark, thus the name.

The range is large and extends east of the Rocky Mountains and south to Texas and into Florida. Host plants include nettles, blackberries, elms, and related trees.

11 APPLIQUÉ PIECES

COLOR NOTES
I used a mottled rusty orange for the forewings, black for the hind wings and body, and violet for the wing edges.

CONSTRUCTION TIP
Each of the wings was sewn off the background then appliquéd as one unit.

DETAILS
Blotches: painted with black brush tip pen

Antennae: stem stitched with two strands of black floss

Veins: quilted in black quilting thread

Size 2½" to 3"

The wings of this butterfly are broad with the forewings extending into rounded hooks on the front edges. The hind wings have a tail that is similar to that of the swallowtail. The wings are a rusty red or orange. The forewings are brighter in color than the hind wings. These butterflies are striped horizontally with brown, and the tails are edged in brown.

They range from the Everglades in south Florida north to the Florida Panhandle and to east Texas. Their host plant is the ficus tree.

5 APPLIQUÉ PIECES

COLOR NOTES
I used two shades of rusty red. The forewings and body are brighter than the hind wings.

DETAILS
Antennae: stem stitched with two strands of floss that matches the body

Stripes: painted with a brush tip pen

Veins: quilted in brown quilting thread

Ruddy Daggerwing

Goatweed

Size 2½" to 3"

The shape of the wings is unusual with an extended hook on the forewings and a blunt narrow tail on the hind wings. The color is a fiery orange red with dark brown on the wing edges. The inside of the hind wings is pale tan. With these pointed wings and tails and with a brown underside, the goatweed resembles a leaf, making it difficult to see while it's at rest.

It ranges from Michigan south to Georgia and the Gulf of Mexico. The host plant is goatweed.

11 APPLIQUÉ PIECES

COLOR NOTES
I used a rusty red for the wings, beige for the inner part of the hind wings, and brown for the body and wing edges.

CONSTRUCTION TIP
Each of the wings was sewn off the background then appliquéd as one unit.

DETAILS
Antennae: stem stitched with two strands of brown floss

Veins: quilted in brown quilting thread

Florida Leafwing

Size almost 3"

This butterfly is also called the Florida goatweed butterfly. It is similar to the goatweed butterfly with its hooked forewings, but it has a smaller tail, and it is brighter in color, a bright red orange. The forewings are brighter than the hind wings, and there are black crescent-shaped markings on the forewings.

Its range is Florida, mostly in the south and including the Keys. Its host plant is the croton.

5 APPLIQUÉ PIECES

COLOR NOTES
I used two shades of red orange, the darker shade for the hind wings. The body is brown.

DETAILS
Crescent-shaped markings: satin stitched with two strands of brown floss

Antennae: stem stitched with two strands of brown floss

Veins: quilted in brown quilting thread

Florida Leafwing

SWALLOWTAILS

The swallowtails are easily recognized because of their bright coloring, shape, and size. These are among the largest of the butterflies with a wingspan up to 5 1/2". They are known for their bright stripes and spots of yellow, white, green, or orange, combined with black or brown. Although some of the swallowtails lack tails, most of them do have long tails on their hind wings.

· · · · · · · · · · · · · · · · · · ·

Spicebush

Size 3½" to 4½"

It is also called the green-clouded swallowtail because of its blue green coloring, which differs from other swallowtails. The forewings of this butterfly are black with creamy yellow on the edges. The hind wings are black and green with one bright orange spot on each wing. The body is black.

Its range is the western part of the United States from Washington south through California to Texas. Host plants include the spicebush and sassafras.

9 APPLIQUÉ PIECES

COLOR NOTES

I used three fabrics: black, deep green, and creamy yellow. The hind wings are green and black.

CONSTRUCTION TIP

For the forewings, I sewed pieces #6 and #8 onto yellow-edge pieces #5 and #7, off the background. I then appliquéd them as a unit.

DETAILS

Antennae: stem stitched with two strands of black floss

Spots: French knots with two strands of orange floss

Veins: quilted in green quilting thread

Spicebush

Tiger Swallowtail

Tiger

Size 3¼" to 5½"

These butterflies are black with bright yellow or gold tiger-like stripes. With this coloring, they are easy to spot in our yards. The forewings and hind wings are bright yellow or gold with wide black edges. Each hind wing has a bright yellow or orange spot. The body is black.

Their range is from central Alaska east to the Atlantic and south to the Gulf Coast. The host plants are varied, depending on the area, but include willows, cottonwoods, birches, and ashes.

9 APPLIQUÉ PIECES

COLOR NOTES
I used bright gold and black fabrics for this butterfly.

DETAILS
Spots: satin stitched with two strands of gold floss

Antennae: stem stitched with two strands of black floss

Veins: quilted in black quilting thread

Zebra

Size 2½" to 3½"

Although they are a bit smaller than most swallowtails, they are easy to spot because of their coloring and shape. They are sometimes called the kite swallowtail because of the tri-angular-shaped wings and long tails. The forewings are zebra-striped black and white. The hind wings are white with a wide black border and bright red on the inner edges. The body and the long tails are black.

They range east of the Mississippi in the southern states. They prefer wooded areas and wet spots, but they do visit our suburban gardens. Their host plant of choice is the paw-paw tree.

25 APPLIQUÉ PIECES

COLOR NOTES
I used black, white, and red fabrics for this butterfly. For forewing pieces #17 and #18, I cut a black-and-white striped fabric on the diagonal.

CONSTRUCTION TIPS
Although this pattern has the most pieces, if it is worked a section at a time, it won't be difficult.

The forewings can be appliquéd in sequence, or each wing can be worked off the background then appliquéd as a unit.

DETAILS
Antennae: stem stitched with two strands of black floss

Veins: drawn with a black pen

Zebra Swallowtail

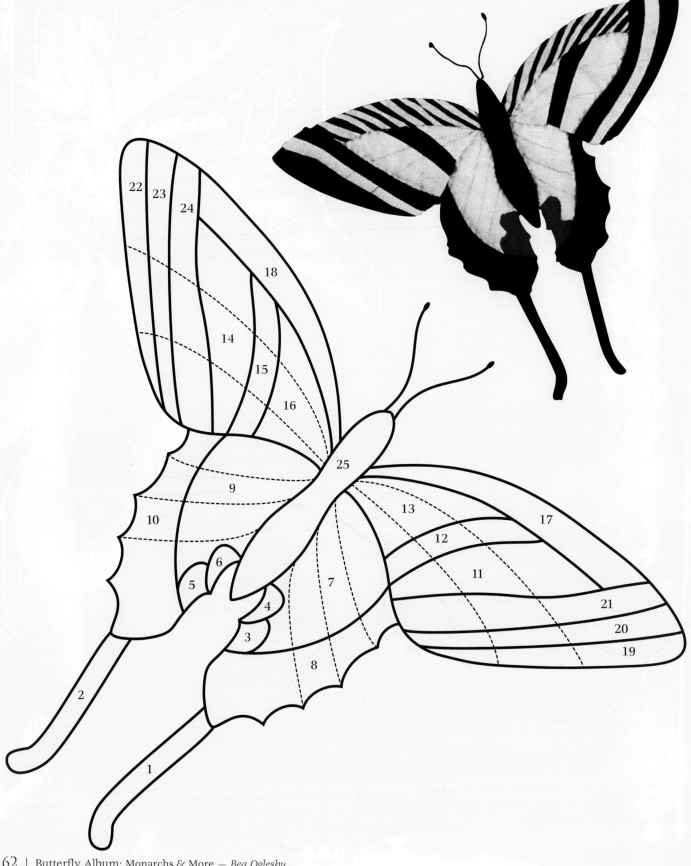

BLUES

In the gossamer wing butterflies, there are four different groups including the blues. The blues are a close relative of the coppers, metalmarks, and harvesters. There are slight variations in their wing shapes, but the blues tend to be blue. These butterflies are very small to medium, but they bring much attention to our gardens because of their color. Every shade of blue is included: dull gray blue, silver blue, marine blue, and greenish blue, in shades both light and dark.

Blues are found in northern as well as southern parts of our country.

• • • • • • • • • • • • • • • • • • •

Blackburn's Bluet

Blackburn's Bluet

Tailed Blue

Size less than 1"

Size about 1"

This butterfly is also called Hawaiian blue. It is one of only two butterflies that are native to Hawaii. Its color ranges from lilac blue to gray blue and even greenish blue.

Its range is restricted to the Hawaiian Islands. The host plant was originally only the koa tree, but it has now adopted other shrubs and tropical plants.

There are eastern and western tailed blues. They are very similar; however, the eastern blue is a fraction smaller and brighter than the western. The body is slate gray. The wings are bright blue edged with silver white.

They range from southern Canada across the United States east of the Rockies. Their host plants are clover, beans, and wild peas.

5 APPLIQUÉ PIECES

5 APPLIQUÉ PIECES

COLOR NOTES

I used two shades of a blue gray fabric for the wings, light for the forewings and dark for the hind wings. A deeper gray was used for the body.

COLOR NOTES

I used two shades of bright blue for the wings, with the deeper shade for the hind wing. A dark gray was used for the body and a silver gray for the wing edges.

DETAILS

Antennae: stem-stitched with two strands of dark gray floss

Veins: quilted in dark gray quilting thread

DETAILS

Antennae: stem stitched with two strands of gray floss

Veins: quilted in light gray quilting thread

Spring Azure

Size ¾" to about 1¼"

Common in the early spring, these butterflies signal the return of warm weather. They are a deep shade of blue edged in black, and they have black bodies.

They are found in the open woods and roadsides, ranging from Alaska east across the entire United States and south to Mexico. Their host plants are many and include dogwood, viburnum, and blueberries.

9 APPLIQUÉ PIECES

COLOR NOTES

I used a marine blue for the wings and navy blue for the body and wing edges.

CONSTRUCTION TIP

The main wing pieces can be sewn onto the edge pieces and appliquéd to the background as a unit.

DETAILS

Antennae: stem stitched with two strands of navy floss

Veins: quilted in navy quilting thread

Marine Blue

Size not larger than 1"

Although this butterfly is included in the blue category, the male is light purple to lavender blue and the female is a dull violet. Their wings are edged with a narrow band of brown.

Their range is in the southwestern states, but they do go north to the central and mountain states in the summer as they follow canals and streambeds. The pea family is their host plant, which includes alfalfa and the sweet pea.

5 APPLIQUÉ PIECES

COLOR NOTES

I used a mottled fabric of light purple or lavender for the wings and a deeper shade for the body.

DETAILS

Antennae: stem-stitched with two strands of floss that matches the body

Wing edges: painted with brown brush tip pen

Veins: quilted in lavender quilting thread

Marine Blue

METALMARKS

There are close to 1,000 species of metalmarks worldwide but only about 24 in North America. Most of these small butterflies are dull in color and come in different shades of gray to rust or brown. The tropical ones can be quite brilliant. The name "metalmark" comes from the shiny metallic markings on their wings. Most of the wings have dark or black spots, and many can be checkered. Not too much is known about these butterflies in North America, and much research needs to be done.

· · · · · · · · · · · · · · · · · · ·

Swamp Metalmark

Size about 1"

With its reddish orange wings and dark brown veins and spots, the swamp metalmark is brighter than other metalmarks. The species is endangered by development.

They live in wet meadows, bogs, and swamps, from western Pennsylvania across the Great Lakes to southern Minnesota. The host plant is the swamp thistle.

5 APPLIQUÉ PIECES

COLOR NOTES

I used a patterned fabric of tan, red, orange, and brown for both the forewings and the hind wings. I used deeper brown for the body.

DETAILS

Wing spots: marked with brown pen

Antennae: stem stitched with two strands of floss that matches the body

Veins: drawn with brown pen then quilted in rust quilting thread

Swamp Metalmark

SATYRS

There are about 50 butterfly species of the satyrs in North America. They are also known as browns. Their color is dull brown or gray. Although most satyrs look dingy, many of the species have eyespots on their wings, giving them a unique look. Eyespots divert predator attacks from their bodies. The satyrs have an erratic flight and do not wander far. They mostly fly at dusk and are frequently mistaken for moths.

• • • • • • • • • • • • • • • • • • •

Alberta Arctic

Alberta Arctic

Size ½" to just under 2"

The Alberta Arctic is typical of the satyrs in color, which is a dull brown or gray brown, but some have a reddish tinge to them. The hind wings are usually a lighter shade then the forewings. They have eyespots of a deeper shade on their wings, with larger spots on the forewings and smaller ones on the hind wings. Some of the eyespots have white "pupils." The body is a deeper brown than the wings.

They range from the prairies in the Dakotas and Montana south to Arizona and New Mexico. Their host plants are native grasses, including fescues.

5 APPLIQUÉ PIECES

COLOR NOTES

I used two shades of reddish tan for the wings, a darker shade for the forewings and lighter for the hind wings. A deeper brown was used for the body.

DETAILS

Wing eyespots: marked with brown pen

Antennae: stem stitched with two strands of reddish brown floss

Veins: drawn with brown pen then quilted in brown quilting thread

Spots: marked with brown pen

COPPERS

The coppers are part of the gossamer wing species, which include the blues, hairstreaks, and the distinctive harvesters. These butterflies are usually bright orange or copper colored; however, they can also be brown, gray, blue, green, purple, or fiery copper. The coloring comes from the different scales in the gossamer wings: the brown, gray, and orange are from pigmented scales; and the blue, green, and purple are from light refracting scales. All of the coppers have basically the same shaped wings with minor variations.

Most are found in the South, but the blues and some copper-colored ones can be found in the North.

• • • • • • • • • • • • • • • • • • •

Purplish Copper

Purplish Copper

Size 1" to 1¼"

This is a medium-sized copper. The color is difficult to describe. Although it is called purple, it is actually a dull brown or gray with purple reflections in the wings. The forewings are darker with the purple, and the hind wings lighter and more gray. Both the forewings and hind wings are edged in light gray with a pink tinge.

It ranges from the Great Lakes and the Midwest prairies west to the Pacific coast. The host plant is the buckwheat family, such as sorrel and dock.

9 APPLIQUÉ PIECES

COLOR NOTES
I used a deep purple for the forewings, dark gray for the hind wing, and light gray for the wing edges.

CONSTRUCTION TIP
I found it easier to appliqué the main wing pieces onto the narrow edges, then treat the wings as a unit to appliqué them onto the background.

DETAILS
Antennae: stem stitched with two strands of floss to match the body

Veins: quilted with quilting thread that matches the wing fabric

Blue Copper

Size 1" to 1¼"

This butterfly can also be included with the blues. The bright sky blue wings are edged with dark brown or black and silver gray. The forewings are usually a bit brighter than the hind wings.

Their range is through the Rockies from Wyoming south to Arizona. They also range west of the Sierra Nevada in California to the coast. The host plant includes several species of the wild buckwheat.

13 APPLIQUÉ PIECES

COLOR NOTES
I used a bright blue for the wings and the body and a deep navy blue and silver gray for the wing edges.

CONSTRUCTION TIP
I found that, with these narrow edges, it is easiest to sew one wing at a time off the background: sew piece #3 onto piece #2. Then sew the joined pieces to piece #1. Appliqué the three wing pieces as a unit to the background.

DETAILS
Antennae: stem stitched with two strands of floss the color of the body

Veins: drawn with deep blue pen then quilted with deep blue quilting thread

Blue Copper

American Copper

Size ⅞" to 1⅛"

The American is the smallest of the coppers. The forewings are bright copper with dark spots and edged with a dark purplish brown. The hind wings are dark purplish brown edged with copper.

Its range is from the East Coast to the mountains in Colorado and south to north Florida. The host plants are sheep sorrel and curly dock in the East and mountain sorrel in the mountains.

COLOR NOTES

Two fabrics were used: a bright mottled copper and a dark purplish brown. The body is dark purplish brown.

DETAILS

Antennae: stem stitched with two strands of floss that matches the body

Veins: quilted in thread that matches the wing fabric

9 APPLIQUÉ PIECES

BIBLIOGRAPHY

Glassberg, Jeffrey. *Butterflies of North America.* Friedman / Fairfax Publishing, 2002.

Mikula, Rick. *Garden Butterflies of North America.* Minocqua, Wisconsin: Willow Creek Press, 1997.

Ordish, George. *The Year of the Butterfly.* New York: Charles Scribner's Sons, 1975.

Pyle, Robert Michael. *National Audubon Society Field Guild to North American Butterflies.* New York: Alfred Knopf, Inc., 1981.

Schappert, Phil. *A World for Butterflies: Their Lives, Behavior and Future.* Buffalo, NY: Firefly Books Ltd., 2000.

Schneck, Marcus. *Butterflies: How to Identify and Attract Them to Your Garden.* Eammaus, Pennsylvania: St. Martin's Press, 1990.

Stokes, Donald & Lillian and Ernest Williams. *Stoke's Butterfly Book.* Boston: Little, Brown and Co., 1991.

Tilden, James W. and Arthur Clayton Smith. *A Field Guide to Western Butterflies.* Boston: Houghton Mifflin Company, 1986.

The Xerces Society / The Smithsonian Institution. *Butterfly Gardening: Creating Summer Magic in Your Garden.* San Francisco: Sierra Club Books, 1990.

PINK-EDGED SULPHUR, 15"x 15", made by the author

INDEX

MARINE BLUE, 15"x 15", made by the author

ABOUT THE AUTHOR

Bea Oglesby started quilting in the mid-1980s, with an interest in traditional pieced quilts. After making many of the traditional pieced quilt patterns, she discovered appliqué in the 1990s. She gathers inspiration from the flowers, birds, and butterflies she sees in nature and combines her love of drawing and nature in her appliqué and her quilts.

She teaches, lectures, and belongs to several quilt guilds. She also does volunteer work in her community. Bea lives in Kansas with her husband.

Bea is the author of *Wildflower Album: Appliqué & Embroidery Patterns* (AQS, 2000) and *Birds & Flowers Album* (AQS, 2003).

HOW SWEET IT IS, 17"x 19", made by the author

OTHER AQS BOOKS

This is only a small selection of the books available from the American Quilter's Society. AQS books are known worldwide for timely topics, clear writing, beautiful color photos, and accurate illustrations and patterns. The following books are available from your local bookseller, quilt shop, or public library.

#6211   us$19.95

#6514   us$21.95

Bendedbias
APPLIQUÉ
Linda M. Poole

#6511   us$22.95

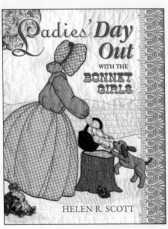

#6676   us$24.95

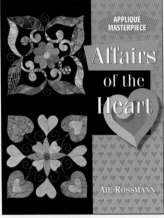

#6517   us$21.95

#5763   us$21.95

#6300   us$24.95

#6004   us$22.95

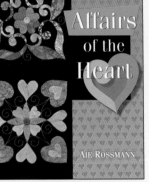

#6410   us$19.95

LOOK for these books nationally.
CALL or VISIT our Web site at

1-800-626-5420
www.americanquilter.com